Let's Get S

Come visit us for ideas of fun learning activities you can do at home with your kids.

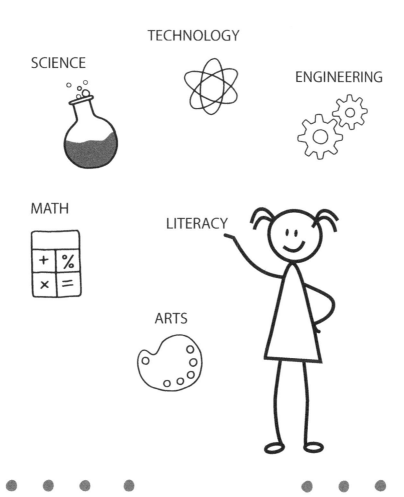

SCIENCE

TECHNOLOGY

ENGINEERING

MATH

LITERACY

ARTS

follow us

 creativitybuilders

 creativitybuilder

email us

hello@creativitybuilders.com
and receive a freebie!

creativity Builders

MY JOURNAL

My name is _____

and I am _____ years old.

THINGS I'LL NEED:

- Pencil
- Crayons or colored pencils
- A positive attitude
- Lots of imagination
- To do my best! ☆

You are embarking on an adventure of a lifetime to find hidden treasure! You have to pack light. What 5 things would you take?

If you were granted 3 wishes...but you could only use those wishes for someone else, what would you wish for?

Write a short story with these 5 words: stinky, star, disappear, gloopity-glop, chicken.

Would you rather have the ability to create fireworks or to control the weather? Why?

Pretend you are suddenly all over the newspapers, TV, radio and internet. What did you do that caused all this media attention?

If there were a new kid in your class or neighborhood, how would you make him or her feel welcome?

Which do you think is more important for kids to learn - sports or the arts? Why?

If your family had to say yes to everything you asked for during an entire day, explain what you would do on "Yes Day".

What is your dream job?

Explain why kids in your class should not have homework. Name at least 3 reasons.

Write about a time you felt like quitting, but you didn't. What did you do to motivate yourself to keep going?

FAIL,
LEARN,
try again

What do you think is more important - space exploration or deep-sea exploration? Explain your choice.

Pretend that you are the teacher for the day. What activities would you ask your classmates to do?

Who is one other kid who inspires you?
How do they inspire you?

One day you go to an antique store and find an amazing _____. You rush home with it, but to your surprise it _____!
What happens next?

_____

_____

_____

_____

_____

_____

_____

_____

ANTIQUES

Which two characters from different shows or books do you think would be great friends? Why?

What if you were in charge of planning the school lunch at the cafeteria for one day? Describe 3-4 different dishes you would choose.

What are some ways you can show love to people around you?

You used a new toothpaste and all of a sudden you cannot speak English anymore! For the rest of the day you are speaking a language that nobody understands. Describe your day.

When are you the most proud of yourself? Why?

I am so
PROUD
of *me*

Imagine a town where everyone looked the same, lived in the same houses, drove the same cars and wore the same clothes.
Describe a day in the life of that town.

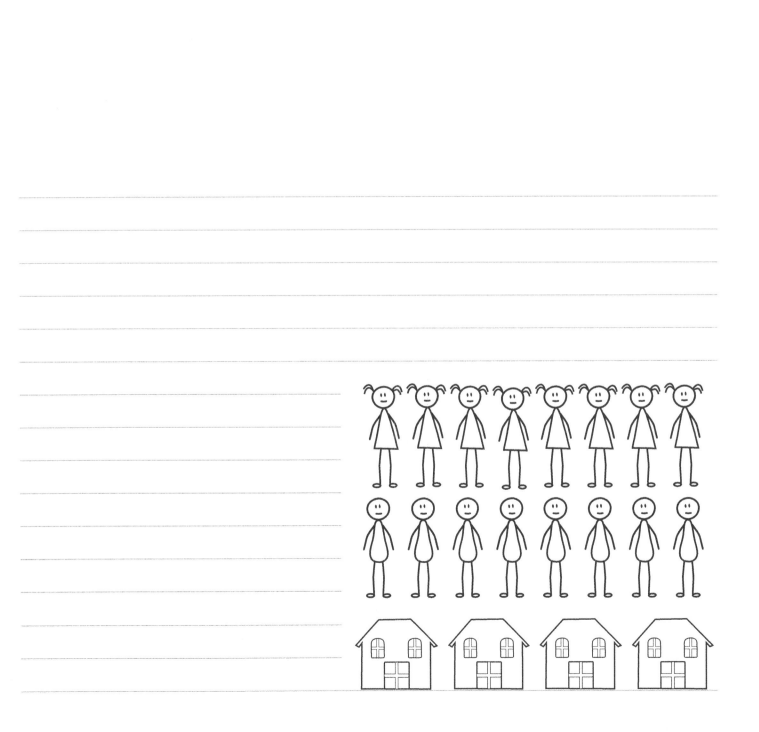

Do you think humans should think of ways to colonize another planet? Why or why not?

Name 5 qualities of a good leader.

A GOOD LEADER...

Imagine you won $5,000 for travel!
Where would you go, who would you take and what would you do?

Write a poem about your favorite food. You can make it funny or really dramatic.

Imagine you are the giant from Jack and the Beanstalk. Explain why the giant is misunderstood and has been the good guy all along.

FEE

FI

FO

FUM !

Make up a new National Holiday and explain when it takes place and how you celebrate it.

Save the Date

Can you think of a time when you were excited to try a new sport, game or other activity? Were you good at it right away or did you need practice to get better?

_____

_____

_____

_____

_____

_____

_____

_____

_____

_____

_____

PRACTICE
makes
PROGRESS

What is one book that you would recommend every kid to read? What makes it so special?

If you could relive one day of your life, what day would it be? Explain your choice.

How would a really good friend describe you?
How would you describe yourself?

Legend says that there is a pot of gold at the end of a rainbow guarded by a leprechaun. Write a story about the leprechaun.

Write about a time that you felt brave. What made you nervous or scared? What strategy did you use to overcome your fear?

Do you believe that "honesty is the best policy"? Why or why not?

HONESTY IS
THE BEST POLICY

☐ YES
☐ NO

If you could turn into any type of insect for one day, which one would you pick? Why?

Antennae Exoskeleton

Three body parts

Class: Insecta

Three pairs of legs

The "Magical Creatures Pet Store" held a contest and you won a pet dragon or unicorn. Explain to your parents why keeping this pet would be good for your family.

Describe your last birthday.
How did you celebrate it?

If kids designed a neighborhood park, how would the new park be different than others? How would it be the same?

At what age should kids be allowed to go to a slumber party? Why?

SLUMBER Party

You are on a nature walk and a tree starts talking to you! Describe your conversation.

What is your happy place? If you were feeling down, could you feel better by just imagining you were there?

HAPPY place

Describe your first day ever at your elementary school.

MY
FIRST
DAY
OF
SCHOOL

If you were an inventor, what would you want to invent that could help you, your family or the world?

Write a different ending to one of your favorite movies or books.

new
endings

Would you rather have 1-2 best friends or 10 casual friends? Why?

friend ♡ *friend*

FRIEND   FRIEND
FRIEND FRIEND
FRIEND FRIEND FRIEND
FRIEND FRIEND
FRIEND
FRIEND

Would you rather have a time machine or a teleportation machine? Why?

Time Travel

Instant Travel

Write about a time when you made a great choice.

What outdoor survival skill do you think would be more interesting to learn: identifying plants for food & medicine or tracking animals?

What is one small thing you are thankful for today? What is one big thing you are thankful for today?

A letter arrived addressed to you. It looks yellowed by time, frayed on the folds and you have a feeling it's extremely important. Who is it from and what does it say?

THANK YOU!

We hope you loved our prompt book!
If you can spare a few minutes, leave us a few stars. ☆
It really helps our small business!

Check out our other titles at:
author.to/creativitybuilders

Writing Prompt Books:
- 50 Writing Prompts for Kids: Grades 1-3
- 50 Writing Prompts for Kids: Grades 3-5
- 31 Spooky Writing Prompts for Kids
- 25 Christmas Writing Prompts for Kids: Grades 1-3
- 25 Christmas Writing Prompts for Kids: Grades 3-5
- 50 Summer Writing Prompts for Kids: Grades 2-5

Elementary School Journal with Editing Checklist:
- Draw & Write Primary Composition Notebook: Grades K-2 | Dinosaur
- Draw & Write Primary Composition Notebook: Grades K-2 | Shark
- Draw & Write Primary Composition Notebook: Grades K-2 | Unicorn
- Handwriting Practice Paper: Exercise Book for Grades K-2 | Bacon & Eggs
- Summer Write & Draw Journal for Kids: Grades K-2

Scavenger Hunt Books:
- Go Explore Discover: Scavenger Adventure Book for Kids
- Go Explore Discover Beach Edition: Scavenger Adventure Book for Kids

Other:
- Trace Letters Handwriting Workbook: Alphabet Practice | Forest Animals Coloring Book
- My First Cookbook: 15 Kid Recipes for Pretend Play

Spanish:
- 50 Ideas de Escritura Para Niños (Spanish Edition)
- Anda Explora Descubre: Libro de Búsqueda y Aventura para Niños (Spanish Edition)

Made in the USA
Las Vegas, NV
12 January 2023

65504011R00059